Epictetus'
The Golden Sayings of Epictetus
In Plain and Simple English

BOOKCAPS

BookCaps™ Study Guides
www.bookcaps.com

Table of Contents

ABOUT THIS SERIES 7

1 9
2 10
3 10
4 11
5 11
6 11
7 12
8 12
9 14
10 14
11 15
12 15
13 15
14 16
15 17
16 17
17 18
18 19
19 20
20 21
21 22
22 22
23 22
24 23
25 24
26 25
27 25
28 25
29 26
30/1 27
32 27
33 27
34 28

35..29
36..29
37..30
38..31
39..32
40..32
41..33
42..33
43..34
44..35
45..35
46..36
47..37
48..37
49..37
50..38
51..38
52..40
53..40
54..41
55..42
56..42
57..43
58..44
59..45
60..45
61..46
62..48
63..48
64..48
65..51
66..51
67..52
68..53
69..54
70..55
71..56
72..57

73 57
74 59
75 59
76 60
77 60
78 61
79 62
80 63
81 64
82 66
83 67
84 68
85 68
86 69
87 69
88 69
89 70
90 70
91 71
92 71
93 72
94 74
95 75
96 75
97 75
98 76
99 76
100 77
101 78
102 78
103 79
104 79
105 81
106 81
107 82
108 83
109 83
110 84

111...85
112...86
113...86
114...87
115...87
116...87
117...88
118...89
119...90
120...91
121...91
122...92
123...92
124...93
125...93
126...94
127...95
128...95
129...95
130...96
131...97
132...97
133...98
134...98
135...99
136...99
137...100
138...101
139...102
140...103
141...103
142...104
143...105
144...105
145...106
146...107
147...108
148...108

149 108
150 109
151 109
152 110
153 111
154 112
155 112
156 113
157 114
158 114
159 114
160 115
161 115
162 116
163 116
164 116
165 117
166 117
167 118
168 118
169 118
170 118
171 119
172 119
173 120
174 120
175 121
176 121
177 121
178 122
179 123
180 123
181 123
182 124
183 124
184 124
185 125
186 125

187 126
188 127
189 128

About This Series

The "Classic Retold" series started as a way of telling classics for the modern reader—being careful to preserve the themes and integrity of the original. Whether you want to understand Shakespeare a little more or are trying to get a better grasps of the Greek classics, there is a book waiting for you!

1

Are these the only gifts which God has given us? How can we possibly explain them or praise them enough? If we could only understand them, would we ever stop singing the praises of God and thanking him, both in public and in private, and speaking of his wonderful gifts? Whether we are digging, ploughing or eating, should we not always be singing this hymn:

God is great, because he has given us these tools with which we can work the land: God is great, because he has given us our hands and the ability to eat and digest; he lets us grow and keep breathing whilst we are asleep!

This is what we should always be singing; yes, and also this, the most wonderful hymn of all:

God is great, because he has given us the brain to understand these things, and the ability to use them!

Well then! Seeing as most of you do not understand this, maybe someone should take your place, and praise God on behalf of all men? I am old and lame, so what else can I do but praise God? If I were nightingale, I would praise him like a nightingale does. If I were a swan, I would do it as a swan does. But since I am a thinking entity, I must sing to God: that is my job: I will do it, and I will not abandon it as long as I have permission to carry on, and I call on you to join in with me.

2

So how do men behave? They behave like someone coming back to his homeland who had stopped for the night in a nice inn, a place they liked so much that they wanted to live there.

"My friend, you have forgotten what you were doing! This was not your destination, it was just a stop on the way."

"No, but this is a good place."

"And how many more good places might you go through as you go on your way! You intended to go back to your country, so that your family could stop worrying about you, so that you could do your bit as a citizen, so that you can get married, have children, and work as a public official when it was your turn. You didn't go on your journey to find out the most pleasant places, you were intending to go back to where you were born, the place of which you are a citizen."

3

Try to enjoy all that life has to offer, and share that enjoyment with other men.

4

But there is somebody I must do my best to please, whom I must allow to rule over me, and whom I must obey: that is God, and those who are close to him. He has given me free will, he allows me to rule over myself, and has given me rules so that I will do that in the correct fashion.

5

Rufus used to say, "If you have time to sing my praises, then what I tell you is worthless." This is truly what he said, so that each of us who was there, whoever had been accused, he put his finger on the faults of each one of us.

6

But what does God say? "If it were possible, Epictetus, I would have made both your body and your possessions completely free, but as things are as they are, do not deceive yourself. Your body does not belong to you, it is just well shaped clay. Since I could not make you completely independent, I have given you a part of myself, I have given you the power to desire, to reject, to pursue and to avoid, in other words I have given you the power to deal with everything relating to the senses. And if you don't forget this, but place all your faith in that, nothing will ever stop you; you will never be sad; and you will neither blame nor praise anyone else for what happens to you. What do you think? Do you think this is nothing?"–God forbid!–"So be happy with it!" And so I pray to the Gods.

What did Antisthenes say? Did you never hear it? He
said, "Oh Cyrus, it is a good thing for a king to do the
right thing and to hear men speak badly of him."

"Yes, but to lower myself like that would be
unworthy of me."

"That," Epictetus said, "is something you to think
about, not me. You know what you think your own
worth is; you know the value you place on yourself.
Men sell themselves for different prices. That was
why, when Florus was debating as to whether he
should appear in Nero's shows as an actor, he asked
Agrippinus why he was not going to appear, and he
replied, 'Because I don't even have to think about my
answer.' Once a man has even started considering
such things, and to work out what the benefit or loss
might be, he is not far from forgetting what sort of
man he is. Why, what is it you are asking me? Is it
better to live or die? I tell you, to live. To have plain
or pleasure? I tell you, pleasure."

"Well, if I don't join in, I will be executed."

"Then go and act! But as for me, I won't do it."

"Why not?"

"Because you are thinking of yourself as like a single thread amongst the many which make up a piece of clothing. You should just try to be like all the rest, in the same way that a single thread doesn't want to be different to any of the others. But I want to be the purple thread–the small shining piece which makes everything else seem so lovely. So why are you asking me to do what everyone else does? That would stop me from being an individual."

9

If men could truly realise, as they should, that we are all created specially by God, and that God is the father of men as well as of gods, he would surely never think badly of himself. Think, if you were adopted by Caesar, you would become intolerably arrogant; so can't you be happy knowing that you are the son of God? However, this is not how we see things nowadays: when we are born we are a mixture of two things, the body which we share with the animals, and the power of reasoning and thinking which we share with the Gods; many people veer towards the dumb animals, few act according to their blessed inheritance from God. Since everyone deals with things according to the way in which he thinks about it, those few people who believe that they have been born to be loyal, modest and to see things as they really are, never think of themselves as in any way low or common, but most people are the opposite. They think that they are just a wretched individual, with a miserable body. It certainly is miserable! But you have something better than that weak flesh of yours. So why do you hold onto the low things and ignore the high?

10

You are just a poor soul trapped inside a dead body.

11

The other day I ordered that an iron lamp should be placed on the altar in my house. I heard a noise at the door and when I hurried down I found that someone had stolen my lamp. I thought that I didn't have to look far to see what would happen to the thief. "Tomorrow, my friend," I said, "you will find a lamp made of clay; whatever a man has, all he can do is lose it.

12

The reason I lost my lamp was because the thief kept a sharper eye out than I did. However, he had to pay a price for that lamp, because to get it he had to become a thief; so the price he paid was that he became a criminal.

13

But God created man to look at Him and His work; not just being a spectator, but also to try and understand them. So it is shameful if a man only behaves like an animal would. That is where he should begin, but he should only stop when he has found those things which nature has placed in us: that is the power of contemplation, understanding, and of living a life which is in harmony with nature.

So make sure that before you die you have understood these matters.

14

You travel to Olympia to see the work of Phidias; each of you thinks it would be a bad thing not to have seen them before you die. But you don't have to travel, you are right here, with the work of God in front of you, aren't you going to bother to look at and think about these?

Do you not want to see who you are or why you were born: or why you have been given the power of thought?

"Yes, but in this life there are some things which are unpleasant and difficult."

And there's nothing unpleasant or difficult at Olympia? Aren't you bothered by the heat? Aren't you crushed in the crowd? Isn't it uncomfortable when you go to bathe? Do you get soaked when it rains? Don't you have to put up with the noise and the shouting and that sort of annoyance? Well, I suppose you weigh this up against the wonderful sights and tolerate it. So what? Haven't you been given a great heart, courage and strength? What do I care, if I have a strong heart, for everything that happens to me? What can knock me down or upset me? What causes me pain? Shouldn't I use the power I have been given for the purpose it has been given to me, instead of moaning and wailing about what happens?

15

If what the philosophers say about the relationship between God and Man is true, then all men should have the same attitude as Socrates: when asked what one's country is, one should never answer, "I am an Athenian or a Corinthian," but, "I am a citizen of the world."

16

Someone who has realised the way the world is ordered, who has learned that the community made up of God and men is the most important, the greatest and most far reaching of all; that the spark of life has come down from God, not only to my father and grandfather but to everything that has been born and grows on earth. A special spark has been given to those who have reason (for they are the only ones whom nature has given the power to converse with God, because reason is what links them to him)–why doesn't someone like that call himself a citizen of the world? Why doesn't he call himself a son of God? Why should anything that men can do worry him? Does being related to Caesar, or to any other of the great men of Rome, free men from all their worries? But if you have God as your Maker, your Father and your relation, surely this would do that?

17

I don't think that an old chap like me should have to sit here trying to stop you thinking badly of yourselves or talking about yourselves in a disparaging manner. However, I want to stop any of you young men, once you recognise that you are related to the Gods and that you are imprisoned by your body and its demands, wanting to shed your body as too great a burden, and leave your family. This is the struggle which your Master and Teacher, if he deserves those titles, should be fighting. You would come to me and say, "Epictetus, we can't stand being imprisoned inside this wretched body any more, having to feed it, water it, give it sleep and purify it, and because of its demands we have to bow down to this man and that. Shouldn't we care nothing for these things? Isn't it true that death is not evil? Aren't we related to the Gods, haven't we sprung from them? Let us go back where we came from: let us be released from these chains which bind us. There are thieves and robbers and courts here on earth, and there are the tyrants, who say that they have power over us because of our miserable bodies and their needs. Let us show them that they have no power at all."

18

This is my answer: "My friends, you must wait for God. When he gives you his signal, and says your time here is at an end, then you can go to him. But for now, you must put up with the position in which he has placed you. You are only here for a short time, and it is an easy thing to tolerate for those who want to. However tyrant, a thief, or a court worry anybody who thinks their body is worthless? Stay here, don't leave before your time!"

19

That is the sort of thing that a teacher should say to innocent young men. As it is, what happens? The teacher is a lifeless body, and so are you. When you have eaten enough today, you sit down and worry about how you are going to eat tomorrow. You are a slave! If you have food, then that is good; if you don't, you will die. The door to heaven is open–why should you be sad? What reason is there for tears? Why should you flatter each other? Why should you beat one another? Why should you be in awe of the rich and powerful, especially if they are also strong and volatile? Why, what can they do to us? What they can do, we will ignore: what we care about, they can't affect. So how can anyone who thinks in that way be ruled over?

20

So seeing this, and seeing the capabilities that you have, you should say, "Oh God, send me any trial you wish; I have the abilities and powers given to me by you to come honourably through anything that happens!" But no, you sit there, trembling with worry that certain things should happen, and then moaning and groaning and sorrowing over what happens. And then you criticise the gods. If you are so mean in spirit then there can only be one result, and that is impiety.

But God has not only given us these powers which mean that we can cope with everything which happens without being crushed or depressed by it; like a good King and Father He has given us these powers without any reservations, to use exactly as we wish, without holding back any power to block us for himself. But although you freely possess all these powers and can use them in whatever way you want, you do not! You don't see what you have been given, nor where it comes from, you sit there moaning and groaning. Some of you do not see where your power comes from, and do not give any thanks to your benefactor; others complain and accuse God in a very degraded fashion.

I can easily show you the abilities which you have been given which will allow you to the brave and great hearted; the powers you have for criticism and accusations, you will have to show me!

21

How did Socrates behave with relation to all this?
How else could he behave but as someone who was
completely certain that he was related to Gods?

22

If God had made the part of his own nature which he
took from himself and gave to us susceptible of being
controlled by either Himself or anyone else, he would
not have been God, nor would he have been looking
after us in the way he should… If you can make
choices, then you are free; if you can make choices,
you cannot blame anyone else–you cannot accuse
anyone else. Everything will happen according to
your wishes and to those of God.

23

There are two ways in which the development of man can become stuck. Firstly his understanding can stall; the same thing can happen to his sense of shame. This happens when a man completely refuses to recognise simple truths, and insists on carrying on believing in something which is clearly untrue. Most of us live in dread of our bodies suffering, and we would make any effort we can to avoid it. But we completely ignore the suffering of the soul. If a man gets into such a state that he can't follow or understand anything, I admit that we do then think that he is in a bad way. But if he ignores all the demands of shame and modesty, we say that he is strong minded!

If we paid as much attention to our business as the old fellows of Rome do to the things that interest them, then we might have achieved something. I know a man who is older than I, now superintendent of the corn market at Rome, and I can remember when he came back this way from exile, telling me about the way he had lived before and saying that in the future all he wanted was to spend his last few years quietly and in peace. "How few years I have left!" he cried. I told him, "You won't do that; as soon as you get back to Rome, you'll forget all about it: if you get a chance to get back into the court, you will be glad to elbow your way in and you will find God for it." "Epictetus," he answered, "if you ever see me so much as one foot inside the Court, you can think as badly of me as you wish."

Well, as it turned out, what did he do? Even before he got into the city, he was met by a messenger from the Emperor. He took the message, and forgot about everything he had said. From then on, he has been building up his fortunes every way he can. I would like to stand next to him and remind him what he said when he came through here, and to also remind him how much better I am at seeing the future than he!

So what am I saying? Am I saying that a man should not be active? Far from it! But what other men do and what we do are two very different things… just glance at what they do and you will see that. All day long they do nothing but reckon up their accounts, plan, have meetings to think how they can make the best profit out of dealing in food, land and so on… what I am telling you to do is to examine how the world is ordered, and what place a thinking being has in it: I want you to think of what you are, and how your good and evil sides are made up.

25

A man who most people thought had been unlucky asked me to write to Rome on his behalf; he had been wealthy and powerful, but then lost everything and was living here. So I wrote a letter for him in a humble way. However, when he read the letter, he gave it back to me, saying, "I asked for your help, not for your pity. Nothing evil has happened to me."

26

True teaching will allow you to learn to be satisfied with everything as it happens. And how do things happen? As God has ordered. He has arranged matters so there is summer and winter, plenty and famine, good and bad, everything has its opposite so that the whole will be in harmony.

27

Always think of this, that when you lose any earthly possession you gain something else in its place; if what you gain is more precious, do not think that you have lost anything.

28

With reference to the Gods, there are those who deny that God exists; other people say that He does exist, but is not involved in the affairs of the world and does not plan anything. Others say that He exists and plans things in advance, but only in the great affairs of heaven, not in anything one. Yet another group say that he does influence things on earth as well as in heaven, but only in a general sense, not for each individual person. Then there is a fifth group, which included both Ulysses and Socrates, who cry: "You know everything I do!"

29

Thinking of all these things, a good and true man will
bow down to the One who rules over the universe,
just as good citizens obey the government. Somebody
who wants to be taught should adopt this attitude:
how can I follow the gods in everything; how can I be
happy with the rule of God; and how can I become
free? The person for whom everything happens the
way he wanted it, and whom nobody can hold back, is
truly free. Does this mean that freedom is madness?
God forbid. Madness and freedom cannot exist
together. "But I want everything that I desire to
happen, in the way that I want it." You are completely
mad. Don't you know that freedom is a glorious thing
and incredibly valuable? Wanting my random desires
to be satisfied may not be noble, and might well be
extremely disreputable.

30/1

You must know that it is not simple for a man to
adopt a principle, unless he speaks of it everyday and
hears others speak of it, and practices it throughout
his life.

So what is the punishment of those who do not accept this? Their punishment is that they will remain as they are. Is somebody unhappy at being alone? Let him remain alone. Is someone unhappy with his parents? Let him be a bad son, and grieve over it. Is anyone unhappy with his children? Let him be a bad father. "Throw him into prison!" some might say. What prison should he be thrown into? He should be left where he is, because he is there against his will, and whenever a man is somewhere against his will, he is in prison. So Socrates was not in prison even when they locked him up, because he agreed to be there.

Do you know what a tiny speck you are in comparison to the universe? I'm only talking about your body, since in terms of intelligence you are equal to, and as important as, the Gods. Intelligence is not measured by size, but by strength of mind. Take your happiness from that virtue which makes you equal to the Gods.

When he was asked how the Gods would like to see a man eat, Epictetus replied: "If when he eats he can be fair, cheerful, sharing, moderate and well mannered, then won't this be acceptable to the Gods? But when you call for hot water, and your slave does not answer, or brings you lukewarm water, or can't even be found, then don't the Gods find it good when you don't explode with anger?"

"But how is one to tolerate such people?"

You awful man, once you show toleration towards your own brother, who has God as his ancestor and comes from the same family, the same high birth, as you? And if you are given a high place in society, does that give you the right to the tyrant? Remember who you are, and who you rule over, remember that they are naturally your family, your brothers, the children of God.

"But I bought them, they didn't buy me."

Do you see where you are taking inspiration from? You are looking down to hell, to the horrible laws of the dead. You're not looking up to the laws of the Gods.

35

When we are invited to a banquet, we take what we are given; if somebody demanded that his host put fish or sweet things on the table he would be thought of as ridiculous. But when it comes to the Gods we ask them to give us what they have not given; we do this even though they have given us so many things!

36

When he was asked how a man can be certain that everything he did was watched by God, Epictetus replied, "Don't you believe that everything on earth and in heaven works together as part of a whole?"

"I do," the person replied.

"Otherwise how would trees be able to flower so regularly, as though ordered by God; how would they be able to send out shoots, to bear fruit, for it to ripen; how would they be able to let their fruit drop and lose their leaves, and fold up and rest? How would we be able to see such changes, such taking turns, on earth as we see in the sky with the moon waxing and waning and the sun approaching and receding?

"So if all growing things, even our own bodies, are tied up with the whole, this is even more true with reference to our souls? And if our souls are tied so firmly to God, actually being pieces of himself, won't he feel every movement of those pieces as if he were moving himself, as if they were part of his own nature?"

37

"But," you say, "I can't take all of this in at once."

"Why, did anyone tell you that you were as powerful as God?"

But God has given each man a Guardian Spirit, whose orders are to watch over him–a Guardian who does not sleep and cannot be deceived. What better or more alert Guardian could he have given us? So when you have shut the doors and everything inside is dark, remember that you should never say that you are alone; you are not alone, God is with you, and your Guardian Spirit; what light do they need to be able to see what you're doing? You should have sworn your loyalty to this God, just as soldiers swear their loyalty to Caesar. When they are signed on, they swear that the life of Ceasar will be more important to them than anything else: will you not swear an oath to God, when he has found you worthy of having so many wonderful gifts? And when she keep your oath once you have sworn it; and what those will use where? You should swear that you will never disobeyed, never complain about anything that he sends to you: you should never be unwilling to do or to suffer anything which comes your way.

"Is this oath like the one they make?"

They swear that no one will be more important to them than Caesar; you swear that our true selves will be more important than anything else.

38

"How can I stop my brother being angry with me?"

___

Bring him to me, and I will stop him being angry. But I'm not going to talk to you about it.

Somebody came to ask Epictetus for his advice, saying, "What I want is that even though my brother won't talk to me, I want to remain just as nature intended."

Epictetus answered, "All great things grow slowly; this is true even about grapes or figs. So if you say to me now, I want to think, I will say to you, you'll have to wait: first it has to flower, then blossom, then ripen. Just as a fig doesn't suddenly become full-grown in a single hour, you can't expect to be able to get the fruit that comes from the mind of man so quickly? Don't expect it, even if I told you to!"

Epaphroditus had a shoemaker whom he sold as being useless. In some way this fellow was later purchased by one of Caesar's men, and started making shoes for Caesar. You should have seen how respectful Epaphroditus became to him then. "How are you, good Felicion? Do tell me!" And if anyone asked, "What is Epaphroditus doing?" The answer was always, "He is asking Felicion about his opinion on such and such." Didn't he sell him for being useless? How had he suddenly decided he was a wise man?

This is what happens when you think that other things besides the Will of God are important.

41

If there is something you won't do yourself, don't try to impose on other people. If you don't want to be a slave, then be careful about enslaving others! If you don't mind making other people slaves, people would think that at one time you must have been a slave yourself. Just as vice and virtue are completely different, so freedom has nothing in common with slavery.

42

What happens when a man is made into a Tribune?
Everyone he meets congratulates him. One man will
kiss his eyes, another will kiss his neck, and the
slaves kiss his hands. He goes home and finds torches
burning outside his house; he goes up to the Capitol
and makes a sacrifice. Did anyone ever make a
sacrifice for the right reasons, knowing that he was
doing just what nature wanted him to do? Really, we
must thank the Gods for those things which make us
happy.

43

Today a man was talking to me about the priesthood
of Augustus. I said to him, "Don't bother with that,
my good sir; you will spend a lot of money for
nothing."

"But it would mean my name would be written on all
documents and contracts."

"Will you be standing by when people read them, to
tell them, 'That is my name written down there?' And
even if you could do that now, what will happen
when you are dead?"

"In any event my name will still be there."

"Write it down on a stone and it will still be there. Think about it, how will anyone remember you outside Nicopolis?"

"But I will be able to wear a golden wreath."

"If you insist on having a wreath, get one made of roses and wear that; you will look more elegant!"

44

Above all else, remember that the doorway to death is always open. Don't be any more afraid than a child; when they get tired of the game, they cry out, "I won't play any more;" in the same way, when you have had enough, cry out, "I won't play any more" and leave. But if you stay, don't complain about it.

45

Is there smoke in the room? If there's only a little, I will stay; if it's thick, I will leave. You must always remember this, hang onto it, the door to death is always open.

"You are not allowed to live at Nicopolis!"

Very well then.

"Nor at Athens."

Then I won't live at Athens either.

"Nor at Rome."

I won't live at Rome either.

"You shall live in Gyara!"

That's that: but to have to live in Gyara seems to me
like being in a room full of choking smoke; I shall
leave to go to a place where no one can forbid me
living: that place is open to everyone! As for my last
piece of clothing, that is my poor body; once you
have taken that, you can't do anything else to me.
That's why Demetrius said to Nero, "You can threaten
me with death, but it is Nature who will punish you!"

46

The first thing a philosopher needs is to be aware of his own state of mind. If a man realises that his mind is weak, then he won't want to use it to think about the most important questions. As it is, men who couldn't cope with reading a sentence buy enormous books and try to swallow the lot. This either makes them throw them up again, or they get indigestion, which gives them cramps, diarrhoea and fever. They should have stopped beforehand and thought about what they could cope with.

47

In theory somebody who is ignorant should be easy to convince: in reality, they don't want to be convinced, and if they are then they hate the man who has convinced them. That's why Socrates said we should always closely examine our own lives.

48

That's why Socrates, when he was told that he should get ready for his trial, answered, "Don't you think I have been getting ready for it my whole life?"

"How have you been doing that?"

"I have always start with what was inside me!"

"What do you mean?"

"I have never, secretly or openly, done anyone any harm."

49

So what sort of person are you being now?

I am a witness whom God has summoned. "Come," God says, "and be a witness for me, you are good enough for that. Is there anything good or bad which you cannot control. Do I do any man any harm? Have I given the power of doing good to any man except to himself? What do you say on behalf of God?"

"I am in a terrible way, Master, I am lost! Nobody cares about me, nobody gives me anything: everybody blames me, everybody speaks badly of me."

Is this how you will speak for God, disrespecting the one who asked you to speak for him, because he has done you the great honour of saying that you are worthy of speaking out for him?

You want men to speak well of you? Then speak well of them. When you have learned to speak well of them, try and do good things for them, and so you will get the reward of them speaking well of you.

When you telling to see any great man, remember that there is someone up above who sees what's going on, and it is him you should be trying to please, rather than any man. So he asks you:

"In your Schools, what did you call exile, imprisonment, chains, death and dishonour?"

"I call them unimportant things."

"So what do you call them now? Have they changed?"

"No"

"So have you changed?"

"No."

"So then, what are unimportant things?"

"Things that we have no control over."

"So tell me, what do you deduce from this?"

"That things which we cannot control are unimportant to me."

"So tell me what things you think good."

"A correct will, and a correct use of the senses."

"And what is your purpose?"

"To follow you!"

52

"How terrible that Socrates should ever have been treated like this by the Athenians!"

You fool! Why do you say "Socrates"? Say it how it is: how terrible that the worthless body of Socrates should have been dragged away and thrown into prison! That hemlock should have ever been given to the body of Socrates; that this body breathed its life away! Does this astonish you? Do you think it is unfair? Is this why you attack God? Did Socrates get no compensation for this? Where was perfect goodness for him then? Who should we listen to, you're him? What does he say?

"Anytus and Melitus can put me to death: however, they do not have the power to harm me."

And also: "If this is what God wants, let it happen."

53

Now, young man, for heaven's sake, now you have
heard these words, go home and say to yourself, "It is
not Epictetus who has told me these things; how
could he? No, it is some kind of God speaking
through him. Otherwise he would never have thought
of saying it to me; he doesn't usually speak to anyone
like that. Well then, do let us suffer the wrath of God,
but let us obey him." Indeed; but if a raven gives you
any message through its croaking, it isn't the raven
but God who is speaking to you through the raven. If
he tells you anything through the voice of a man, isn't
it him who is making the man say these things to you,
so that you can know his divine power–he sends signs
to some people in one way and to others in another,
and in the most important matters he shows what he
has ordered through his highest messengers?

What else could the poet mean:

First I spoke to him myself, and I sent
Mercury, the shining one, to stop him and to warn
him,
Not to kill the husband, or to seduce the wife.

54

The same applied to my friend Heraclitus, who had some unimportant lawsuit going on about a little farm near Rhodes. To begin with he demonstrated to judges that he was in the right, and then he finished up by crying, "I'm not going to beg you, and I don't care what you decide. It's you who are on trial, not me!" And that was how he finished his case.

55

As for us, we carry on like a herd of deer. When they run away in fright from the arrows of the huntsman, which way do they go? What safe place do they rush to? Why, they charge straight into the net! And so they die by confusing safety and things which they fear… You should not fear death or pain, you should only be afraid of your fear. The poet was right when he wrote:

Death is nothing to be afraid of; you should only be afraid of a shameful death!

56

So why do we say that certain things are natural, and others are against nature?

Well, just as we might describe ourselves if we stood alone and apart from other people. I would agree that it is natural for a foot to be clean. But if you regard it as part of a body, not something just on its own, it is good for it (if it needs to) to walk through the mud, to tread on forms, sometimes even to be amputated, so that the whole body can benefit; otherwise it would no longer be a foot. That is how we should think about ourselves. What are you? You are a man. If you are viewed in isolation, it is natural for you to live long, enjoying health and wealth. But if you looked at as a Man, a part of a Whole, sometimes for the sake of the Whole at one point you may have to fall ill, at another risk the dangers of the sea, perhaps at another time to be deprived and even die an early death. So why do you despair? Do you not know that just as an amputated foot is no longer a foot, if you were taken away from Mankind you would no longer be a man? For what is a man? He is a part of the city; firstly of the city of Gods and men; then he is a part of his city on earth, which is a copy of the heavenly city of about as part of such a group, in the world which we all make up, in lives like these, things like this may happen to one person or another. So your choosing, as you are on earth, is to speak correctly about these things, and to follow them in the most fitting fashion.

57

Diogenes made a good reply to a man who asked him for a reference: "When he sees you he will know that you are a man; whether you are a good or bad man, he will know if he has any talents to tell good from bad. But if he doesn't have that talent, he will never be able to see this, even if I wrote him a thousand references." It is as though a silver coin asked somebody to write him a reference to a tester. If the tester knows his job, he will know if it is silver or not: the coin can demonstrate it without any references.

58

Just as a traveller asks people he meets for directions, not wanting to veer off to the left or the right (because he just wants to go straight to his destination), we should approach God as our guide like that. Just the same way we use our eyes, not telling them to show us one thing or another, happy to take in everything they show us. As it is we stand anxiously watching our sacrifice, and in the voice of a beggar we call out to the priest, "Master, please have mercy on me, show me away to escape!" Idiot, do you want anything to happen except that which is for the best? Is there anything better than what God wants? Why would you, as far as you can, try to corrupt your judge, and pervert your counsellor?

59

God is kind. But what is for the best is also a
kindness. So it would appear that where we see the
true nature of God, we can also find the true nature of
what is for the best. So what is the true nature of
God? Intelligence, knowledge and good thoughts.
This is where you should go directly to look for the
true nature of what is for the best. Surely you won't
look for it in a plant or in a dumb animal.

60

So you must look for the true nature of goodness in those things which, if they did not exist, you could not say goodness existed. Well then? Aren't other things apart from humans works of God? They are; but they have a lower position, and they are not parts of God. But you are the thing which is most honoured: you are a piece of God: you have part of him inside yourself. Why then do you not recognise your great ancestry–do you know where you come from? When you eat, won't you remember who you are who is eating, and who you are feeding? When you talk, when you exercise, when you have debates, don't you know that you are feeding a God, exercising a God, the God who you always carry about with you, you miserable man, and you do not see it. Do you think that I'm speaking about God made of silver and gold, outside you? No, you carry him inside you! You don't see how you can lose him with your impure thoughts and unclean deeds. If you had a picture of God in front of you, you wouldn't dare to act the way you do, but with God himself inside you, seeing and hearing everything, it doesn't embarrass you to think such thoughts and do such deeds; you don't recognise your own nature, and so God is angry with you!

So why are we afraid when we send a young man out
from the Schools into society, worrying in case he
makes an exhibition of himself through wearing
ragged clothes or excessive finery? Doesn't he know
he has God inside him, doesn't he know who is with
him as he starts his journey? Should we put up with
him saying, 'I wish you were coming with me!'–
Don't you have God coming with you, and having
him alongside you do you still want somebody else!
Would he tell you anything different to this? Why, if
you were a statue made by Phidias, one of Athena or
Zeus, you would think of both yourself and the one
who made you; and if you had any sense you would
try not to disgrace either yourself or the one who
made you, and never to appear unworthy in the eyes
of those who see you. Is it because God is your maker
that you don't care how you appear? But what a
different case this is! What human artist can include
its own intelligence in the work it makes? Is it
anything except for marble, bronze, gold or ivory?
No, when Phidias' Athena holds out her hand and
wins a victory, she stands in that pose for eternity.
But the works of God move and breathe; they use
their senses and the judge with them. Are you going
to show disrespect for the workmanship of an artist
like that? When he not only made you but handed the
guardianship of yourself to you alone, are you not
only going to forget this, but also show disrespect for
the thing you have been given to look after! If God
had asked you to look after an orphan, would you
have neglected him like this? He has puts you into
your own hands, saying, 'You are like me, and I have
the same faith in you: make sure this man remains as

nature made him–modest, faithful, high-mind and never giving in to fear, passion or anxiety…

This is how I will show myself to all of you.–"What, someone who cannot suffer sickness, or age, or death?"–No, but someone who accepts sickness, accepts death, as a God should!

62

Diogenes tells us that the only good labor is that which strengthens and emboldens the soul, not the body.

63

When a guide finds someone who is lost, he brings him back to the right path-he doesn't mock and jeer at him and then leave. You must also show the uneducated man the truth, and he will follow you. But if you don't show it to him then you shouldn't mock him, you should recognise your own failings.

The most obvious thing which first struck one about Socrates was that he never became angry during discussions, he never said anything hurtful or insulting; on the contrary, he always tolerated insults from other people and so put a stop to the argument. If you would like to know how good he was at this, read Xenophon's Banquets, and you will see how many quarrels he managed to stop. This is why the Poets are right in praising this skill so highly:

He would quickly and also wisely bring even bitter arguments to an end.

However, to do this is not at the moment very safe, especially in Rome. Someone who does this, I hardly need so, shouldn't try and do it in secret, but should, if they get the chance, approach some wealthy or high-ranking person.

"Can you tell me, sir, who looks after your horses?"

"I can."

"Do you trust them to the first person who comes along, who knows nothing about them?"

"Certainly not."

"Well, what about the man who looks after your gold, your silver or your clothes?"

"He must also be an experienced man."

"And your body—have you ever thought of letting someone else look after it?"

"Of course I have."

"And no doubt you thought of handing it over to a person with experience, a trainer or doctor?"

"Of course."

"And these the best things you have, or do you have anything more precious?"

"What on earth are you talking about?"

"I mean that thing which employs these things, which weighs everything up, which dictates what you do."

"Oh, you mean the soul."

"You understand correctly, I do mean the soul. I swear, I value that more highly than everything else I own. So can you tell me how you take care of your soul? It can hardly be possible that a man of your intelligence, so highly regarded in the city, would allow his most precious possession to be ruined through carelessness and neglect."

"Certainly not."

"Well, do you look after yourself? Did anyone teach you how to do it, or did you discover it for yourself?"

This is where it gets dangerous; the great man may answer, "Why, what business is that of yours, my good fellow? Are you my master?" And then, if you carry on bothering him, he may lift up his hand to hit you. It was fine thing to do, I used to think, until that started happening to me.

65

A young man was showing off in the theatre and saying, "I am wise, because I have spoken to many wise men," Epictetus answered, "I have spoken to plenty of rich men, but I'm not rich!"

We can see that carpenter becomes a carpenter by
learning certain things: a pilot on a ship learns certain
things to become a pilot. So it may be in the present
case that simply wanting to be wise and good it's not
enough. Certain things have to be learnt. So this is
what we are looking for. The Philosophers want us to
learn first of all that there is a God, and that he rules
over the universe: furthermore, they want us to know
that to try and hide what one does, and even what one
thinks and intends to do, is impossible. Secondly,
they want us to examine what the nature of God is.
Whatever we find that nature to be, a man who wants
to please him and obey him must try as hard as he can
to be like him. If God is faithful, he must be faithful;
if God is free, he must also be free; if he is generous,
so must the man be generous; if he is tolerant, the
man must be tolerant also. So he must copy God in
everything he does and says.

If I show you that you are lacking in the most important thing to be happy, that up until now you have been focusing on everything other than the most important thing, and that on top of that you have no idea of what God or Man actually are, or what Good or Evil is: you could perhaps stand to be told that you know nothing about everything else, but how can you stand hearing that you know nothing about yourself? Could you possibly stand there whilst that is proved to you? Of course you couldn't. You would turn away angrily at once. But what harm have I done? I could only be doing harm if you can say that the mirror harms the ugly man by showing him his face; it is only an insult if you think the doctor is insulting his patient when he tells him, "My friend, do you think that you are perfectly healthy? You have a fever. You should fast today, and only drink water." But nobody says, "What a terrible insult!" But if you say to a man, "Your passion is raging, your ability to resist temptation is weak, your intentions are foolish, your feelings are not in harmony with nature, your opinions are rash and false," he goes off at once and complains that you have insulted him.

The way we live is like a fair. The flocks and herds of animals are going along to be sold, and most of the people there have come to buy and sell. But there are a few who have just come to look at the fair, to ask why it is being held and how it is organised, who orders it and why. So, in this great Fair of life, some, like cattle, don't care about anything but their fodder. All of you who are spending their time busy with their land, slaves and public office, you should know that this is just the fodder! There are few who are attending the Fair who love to think about what the world is, and who runs it. Is it possible that nobody rules it? Is it possible that although neither a city nor household could last for a minute without someone to rule over it and take care of it, this great universe, so lovely, so huge, could be kept in such wonderful order simply by chance, with no ruling plan? So there has to be someone ruling over it. What is He like, and how does he rule? And who are we, his children, and what were we born to do? Do we have any close connection or relationship with him?

These are what the few people of whom I am speaking think about. Furthermore, all they do is consider and examine everybody there before they leave. Well, most people mock them. This is what the traders do to the observers, and if the animals could talk, they would mock anyone who thought of anything except fodder.

69

I think I now know something which I never knew
before; what the proverb means when it says, "A fool
cannot bend and he cannot break." I pray to God that
I never have a wise fool as a friend! Nobody is so
difficult to budge. "I've made my mind up!" That's
what madmen say; but the more convinced they are
that they are right, the more they need to be treated.

70

"Oh! When will I see Athens and the Acropolis
again?" You miserable man! Aren't you happy with
what you see every day? Can you think of anything
greater or nobler than the sun, the moon and the stars,
than the earth and the sea spread out for you? If you
actually understand the One who rules over the
universe, if you are carrying him about inside you,
how can you still miss pieces of stone and fine rocks?
When you have to say goodbye to the sun and the
moon, will you sit down and cry like a child? Why,
what did you hear, what did you learn? Why did you
say that you were a philosopher, when you could have
written down the truth, which was, "I have put
together one or two books, I have read some of
Chrysippus' works, but I have barely dipped my toe
into the sea of philosophy!"

My friend, before it is too late you should hold on as tightly as you can to freedom, tranquillity and greatness of soul! Look up, like someone who has escaped from slavery; have the courage to look up at God and say, "From now on deal with me as you wish; you and I are thinking the same. I am yours: I will not reject anything that you think is good; take me where you want; dressed me in what clothes you wish; do you want me to be a ruler or subject, to live at home or in exile, to be poor or rich? I will explain all these things to men on your behalf. I will show them the true nature of each one..."

Who would Hercules have been if he had stayed at home? He would not have been Hercules, but Eurystheus. And how many friends and comrades did he make as he wandered through the world? But nothing was dearer to him than God. That made men believe that he was the son of God, as he certainly was. So he wandered the Earth saving people from injustice and lawlessness, showing his obedience to God.

But, you say, you are not Hercules, and you can't save other people from their sins–you're not even Theseus, you couldn't drive the monsters out of Attica. Throw out your own terrors from your mind, not robbers and monsters, but fear, desire, envy, spitefulness, greed, effeminacy, excess. You cannot banish these things unless you focus solely on God, giving him all your love and submitting to his orders. If you do anything else you will be forced to follow a strength greater than your own, sighing and groaning, always looking for something external to bring you tranquillity, and never being able to find it. For you are looking for it where it cannot be found; and where she can be found, you don't look for her!

72

If a man wants to study philosophy, the first thing he must do is to get rid of those preconceptions. It is impossible for a man to learn about something when he believes that he already knows about it.

73

Just give me one young man who has come to the School to learn, who wants to follow this path, and he says, "I give up everything else, I will be happy if I can just spend my life free of trouble or limitations, if I can hold my head high and face the world as a free man and, if I can look up to heaven as a friend of God and be afraid of nothing that may happen!" Show me such a person, so I can say, "Come in, young man, and claim your rights. It is your place to be a philosopher. These things belong to you, these are your books, these speeches!"

And when this champion has immersed himself in this part of the subject, I hope you will come back to me and say, "What I want is to be free from passion and from mental anguish; as someone who will do anything to follow piety and philosophy, what I want is to know what my duties are to the Gods, my parents, my brothers, my country, to strangers."

"So start studying the second part of the subject, that is also yours."

"But I have already mastered the second part; but I want to stand firm and unshaken and, just as much when I'm asleep as when I'm awake, as much when I am happy and drunk as when I am depressed."

"My friend, you are truly a God! You have great plans."

74

"The question in front of us," said Epictetus, "is a great one; it is this: are we sentient beings, or not?"

75

If you have given into anger, you can be certain that apart from the evil involved in doing so, you have made a habit stronger, you have added fuel to the fire. If you give in to the temptations of the flesh, don't think that it's just a single lapse, you have strengthened your bad habits. All habits and your faculties must be affected by the things you do. Ones which did not exist come into being, and the others become stronger and more dominant. This is what philosophers say about diseases of the mind:

Suppose that you lusted after money at one point: if you had enough intelligence to realise that this was evil, then that lust is controlled, and the mind takes back its original authority; however, if this does not happen, the mind will not be able to retake control–on the contrary, the next time it feels the same lust the flame of desire will leap up more quickly than it did before. Through doing things over and over again, in the long term the mind becomes hardened to what it is doing, and so it produces the mental illness of Avarice.

If someone has had a fever, he is not as healthy as he was before even when the disease has left him, unless the cure is really complete. The same is true with relation to diseases of the mind. The scars will still be there, and unless they are effectively wiped out, more blows in the same place well not just produce blisters, but sores. If you don't want to get angry, then stay out of the habit of being angry, don't give your anger any fuel. Begin by keeping quiet and counting the days when you didn't give in to anger: "I used to be angry every day, then it was every other day, then every couple of days, then every three days!" and if you manage to go thirty days without giving in to anger, then make a sacrifice to the Gods in thanksgiving.

76

So how can you get to this place? Make a decision, if you never have before, that you will behave as you know you should; decide that you will behave in such a way that God will be pleased with you; desire to behave in a way so that both you and God will see yourself as pure!

77

The person who trains himself to resist the lure of external temptation is a true athlete.

"Stay, you wretched man! Don't let yourself be dragged away!" This is a great fight, and a Divine task! You are fighting for kingship, for freedom, for happiness and tranquillity. Remember God: call him to help you, like a comrade who stands beside you in a fight.

78

So then who is a Stoic–in the same way that we might call a statue Phidian if it is done in the style of that master? Show me a man who can be called this, who follows the doctrines he is always speaking of. Show me a man who is sick and happy; who is exiled, and happy; who has a bad reputation, and is happy! I ask you again, shaming him. So help me God, I'm dying to see a single Stoic! Well, if you can't show me one who is complete, at least let me see someone who is working towards that, someone who wants to become one. Doing a favour! Don't begrudge an old man the chance to see something he has never yet seen. Do you think I want to see the statues of Zeus or Athena made by Phidias, covered with gold and ivory? No, one of you should show me a human soul who wants to achieving his mind to that of God, do not place blame on God or man, to allow nothing to disappoint him, nothing to block his path, who does not give into envy, anger or jealousy–in a word, why should we pretend otherwise, show me someone who wants to change from a man into a God. Someone who has the purpose, while still imprisoned in this dead body, of becoming equal to God. Show him to me! Ah, you cannot! So why do you make fools of themselves and deceive other people? Why do you walk around dressed in other men's clothes, stealing names to which you have no right!

79

if you have pretended to be someone greater than you are, you have not only acted that part badly, but you have neglected to play the part of which you are actually capable.

80

Now you, at home you have beaten a slave: you have creative chaos in your household, and disturbed your whole neighbourhood. And then you're going to come to me pretending to be modest, and sit down like a wise man and criticise my explanation of texts, saying that my thoughts are just idle babble? Have you come here full of envy, upset because nobody has sent you anything from home? While the discussion is going on, do you sit there thinking about nothing but how your father or your brother are thinking about you, thinking, "What are they saying about me back home? At this moment they think that I am making progress and they are saying, 'He will come back knowing everything!' I wish I could learn everything before I go back, but that would be a real pain to do. Nobody is sending me anything–the baths at Nicopolis are dirty; I hate the way things are at home and I hate it here." And then people will say, "the School does nobody any good." Who is there who comes to the School sincerely wishing to learn, to be ready to give up what he believes and to change as he is ordered? Who comes to discover what he needs? So then why are you surprised if you go back home from the School exactly the same as you came into it?

81

"Epictetus, I have often come here wanting to hear you speak, and you have never said anything to me; now, if possible, I beg you, say something to me."

Epictetus replied, "Do you think that there is an art in speaking as there is in other things, if it is to be done skilfully and do the this is no good?"

"Yes."

"And does everyone profit from what they hear, or only some of the audience? So it seems there is a skill needed for listening as well as for speaking... To make a statue you need to have skill: to view it correctly you also need skill."

"Agreed."

"And I think everyone would agree that the person who wants to listen to philosophers needs to be taught very intensively how to listen. Isn't that the case? Tell me what you think you can hear me talk about."

"Why, about good and evil."

"The good and evil of what? A horse, an ox?"

"No; the good and evil of man."

"So do we know what a man is? What his nature is? What idea we have of him? Do we have any skill in listening about the subject? No, do you understand what nature is? Do you understand at all when I say that I will have to use examples? Do you understand what the use of examples is? What true or false means? Do I have to force you to understand philosophy? Tell me what good my talking to you will do. Make me want to do it. When a sheep sees a field which it loves it wants to feed: if you show it a stone or a bit of bread he doesn't feel anything. As humans we also have certain natural desires, one of which is that we want to speak when we find a listener worthy of us, someone who inspires us. But if the listener just sits there like a stone or a tuft of grass, how can that make a man want to speak to him?"

"So you won't say anything to me?"

"I can only tell you this: someone who doesn't know who he is, or why he was born; someone who doesn't know what kind of world this is and the sort of people here is associated with; someone who cannot distinguish good from evil, beauty and foulness, truth and lies, that person will never develop his reason to shape his desires and impulses and resistance, nor will he be able to make proper judgements; to put it simply, he will walk around deaf and blind, thinking that he is of some consequence, when in fact he is worthless. Is there anything new in what I'm saying? Isn't this ignorance the reason for all mistakes and misfortunes of mankind since the human race began?"

"That's all I have to say to you, and even that I had to force out. Why? Because you have not inspired me. What is there in you which I can see which would inspire me, in the way a good horse inspires a horseman? Your body? You treat it badly. Your clothes? They are extravagant. Your behaviour, your looks? There's nothing there. When you want a philosopher to speak to you, don't complain, "You never say anything to me"; show that you deserve to be spoken to, and then you will see how you inspire the speaker.

82

And now, when you see brothers who are apparently good friends and living in harmony, don't make up your mind about their friendship at once, even if they swear to it, if they declare, "It would be impossible for us to live apart!" The heart of a bad man has no loyalty, no principles, no constancy: at one point it will be swayed by one thing, then by another. Don't ask the normal questions, such as do they share the same parents, did they grow up together, did they have the same teacher. Just ask this, do they invest their efforts truly in their will, or in external things. If the answer is external things, don't call friends, and don't call them loyal, constant, brave or free; if you have any sense you won't even call them human beings… But if you hear that these men believe that goodness is only contained within the will, if they only deal correctly with the right things, don't bother asking if they are father and son or brother is all long-term friends. If you are certain of that one point, you can say with certainty that they are friends, that they are faithful and just. Where else can friendship be found except when there is modesty, when people share only those things which are fair and honest?

83

No man can steal away our Will–no man can ever rule over that!

84

When disease and death catch up with me, I would
like to be found working to free my Will from the
attacks of passion, from the things which block it,
from resentment, from slavery.

This is how I want to be found, so that I can say to
God, "Have I done anything against your commands?
Have I in any way misused the faculties, the senses,
the natural principles that you have given me? Have I
ever blamed you what criticised the way you run
things? When you once it it to happen, I became sick–
and so did other men: I agreed to this. Because it was
what you wanted, I became poor; but my heart was
glad. I gained no political power, because you
decreed I should not; so I never wanted such power!
Have you ever see me looking sadder because of that?
Haven't I always come to you cheerfully, waiting for
your orders, watching for your messages? Do you
now want me to leave this great gathering of men? I
am going: I give you all my thanks, that you thought
that I deserved to be with you in this gathering, to see
your works and to understand your rules."

This is what I would like to be thinking of, writing of
and studying when death comes to me.

85

Do you think that it is nothing to never make accusations, to never blame either God or man? To remain constant under all circumstances? This was the secret of Socrates, but he never said that he knew or could teach anything... Which of you wants to be like this? If you were truly like that, you would happily put up with sickness, hunger and even death.

86

How are we made by nature? To be free, to the noble, to be modest (for what other living creature can blush or feel shame?) and to give up the pursuit of pleasure to follow the purposes for which nature designed us and, as her servant and Minister, to behave in the ways which nature has laid down for us.

87

Farmers deal with their land; doctors and trainers deal with the body; the wise man deals with his own mind.

88

Who amongst us does not admire what the Spartan Lycurgus? A young citizen had cut out his eye, and the people had handed him over to Lycurgus to give him whatever punishment he wanted. He resisted the temptation to punish him, quite the opposite; he taught him and made him into a good man. He showed him to the public in the theatre, saying to the astonished Spartans, "You gave me this young man when he was violent and arrogant; I am giving him back to you in his right mind, he is now fit to serve his country."

89

A money changer cannot refuse to accept the coins of Caesar, nor can a grocer; once he is shown the coin, he must hand over his goods in exchange, whether he wants to or not. This is the same with the soul. Once good appears, it attracts more good; evil is rejected. The soul can never refuse to accept clear goodness, any more than a man can refuse to accept the coins of Caesar. This is the principle which rules over both God and man.

When he was asked what common sense was,
Epictetus answered:

"What is called normal hearing can only make out
different sounds, being able to tell the difference
between musical notes is not normal but comes from
training; so there are certain things which men who
are not entirely perverted can see our natural
principles which we all share. These things in the
mind are called common sense."

91

Can you judge men? Then let us be like you, as
Socrates did. Do this, don't do that or I will throw you
into prison; this is not ruling over men like creatures
who have reason. What you should say is that you
should do as God has ordered, otherwise you will
suffer punishment and loss. You ask what loss will
you suffer? Just this: if you do not do what you
should you will lose the faithfulness, the reverence,
the modesty that you have inside! Don't think that
there is any greater loss than this!

"His son is dead."

What has happened?

"His son is dead."

Nothing more?

"Nothing."

"His ship is lost."

"He has been dragged off to prison."

What has happened?

"He has been dragged off to prison."

Whether any of these things are misfortunes, everyone decides for themselves. But (you say) these things make God unjust. Why? Because he gave you endurance and a great soul? Because he arranged matters so that such things are not evil? Because he made it possible for you to be happy, even when you are suffering these things? For providing you with an exit, when things do not go well for you? Leave, my friend, and stop criticising!

You tell me that you are sailing to Rome to ask for the job of Governor of Cnossus. You aren't happy to stay at home with the honours you already had; you want something bigger, better. But have you ever made a journey in order to look over your own principles and get rid of any which were faulty? Did you ever visit anyone for that reason? Did you ever put any time aside for that? What age will you? Look over what you have done in your life–do it in private, if you are changed to do it in front of me. When you were a boy, did you look at your principles? Didn't you do everything just the same as you do now? Or when you were an adolescent, going to the school of oratory and practising that art yourself, did you ever imagine you lacked anything? And when you were a young man, taking on cases and making a name for yourself, did you think that there was anyone who could equal you? When would you have put up with someone else looking at your principles and showing you that they were faulty? So what do you want me to say to you? "Help me with this!" you cry. Ah, I have no methods for doing that! And if that's what you wanted, you weren't coming to me as a philosopher, you come to me just like any other tradesman. "What can philosophers do then?" Why, whatever happens, the faculties which rule us will remain just as nature wishes. Do you think this is a small thing? It is not! It's the greatest thing there is. Well, can it be picked up in a short time? Can someone just pick it up as they pass by? You try, if you can!"

Then you will say, "Yes, I met Epictetus!"

Yes, just as in the same way you might say that you saw a statue or monument. You saw me! That is all. When a man actually meets a man then he learns what the other one is thinking, and shows him what he is thinking in turn. Explore my mind–show me yours; and then you can say that you met me. Let us examine each other; if any of my principles are faulty, take it away from me; if any of your soul, get rid of them. That is what it means to meet a philosopher. This is not the case, you think; you are just playing a flying visit, thinking that while you are chartering the ship, you can see Epictetus as well! Let's see what he has to say. Then when you leave you cry out, "Damn Epictetus so being a worthless fellow, what he says is provincial and crude!" So what else in fact did you come to judge?

<hr />

94

Whether you like it or not, you are poorer than me!

"So what am I missing?"

The things which you don't have: a stable mind,
which nature desires: tranquillity. What do I care
whether or not I have a patron? But you care. I am
richer than you; I'm not tortured by worries about
what Caesar thinks of me; I don't have to flatter
anybody. This is what I have, instead of gold and
silver cups! Your cups might be made of gold, but
your intelligence, your principles, your ideas, your
inclinations and your desires are all made of pottery.

95

To you, everything you have seems very small: to me,
everything I have seen is huge. Look at children
pushing their hands into a jar with a narrow neck,
trying to pull out the nuts and figs inside. If they take
a fistful, they can't pull it out again and they start
crying. "They go over a few of them, and then you
will be able to pull out the rest!" You must also let go
of your desires! Don't covet too many things, and you
will get the few which you want.

96

Pittacus was done wrong by somebody whom he had the power to punish. But he let him go free, saying it is better to show forgiveness than to take revenge. Forgiveness shows natural gentleness, revenge shows savagery.

97

"My brother should not have treated me like this."

True, but that is his concern. However he treats me, I must treat him properly. This is my duty, and nobody can stop me doing it.

98

Still, a man should be prepared to be enough for himself–to live just with himself, just as God lives alone, sleeps with no one, thinking always of those things which is a suitable for him to think of. So we should be able to talk to ourselves, to need nobody with us, not to wish for any diversions, we should think about the rule of heaven, and how we fit into the great scheme. We should look at how human misfortunes affected us in the past, and how they affect us now; what there is which can still hurt us, and how it can be cured; we must try to make those things which our intelligence can make perfect, perfect.

if a man frequently speaks with others, either in debate, for entertainment, or just friendship, he must either become like them or he must make them like him. If you put a burning coal next to one which has gone out it will either set fire to it or the dead one will put it out. As this is the risk, one should be cautious before forming such friendships, remembering that you can't spend time with a man covered in soot without getting some on himself. What will you do when the conversation turns to gladiators, or horses, or boxers, or (even worse) personalities, condemning one person or another, approving one or another? Whatever man sneers or jeers or shows that he has a bad temper? Are there any of us who have the skill of a lute player, who knows as soon as he touches the strings which ones are out of tune and can rectify it? Do any of you have the power which Socrates had, in all his discussions with men, of winning people over to his own beliefs? No, you are pulled this way and that by uneducated men. How is it that they can triumph over you? It is because they speaking from the heart–their base corrupt views on what they really believe. Your fine words only come from your lips, not your heart; that is why they are so lifeless. It makes one feel sick to listen to your speeches, hearing about your miserable virtue which you won't stop talking about. This is why vulgar people can overcome you.

100

In general, anything which you do to your body which controls its passions is good, if it is done for the sake of discipline. But if you do it to show off, you will immediately be revealed as a shallow man who has an ulterior motive, wanting people to shout out, "O what a great man that is!" This is why the saying of Apollonius was so excellent: "If you want to train yourself privately, wait until some time when you are suffocating from the heat; then take a mouthful of cold water and spit it out again, and don't tell anyone!"

101

Learn how to behave like someone who is ill, so that afterwards you can behave as someone who is healthy. Fast; just drink water; completely shun desire, so that from now on your desires can be controlled by your mind.

102

Do you want to do good for men? Then show them through your own example what kind of men philosophy can make, and stop concerning yourself with foolish things. When you are eating, help those who are eating with you; when you are drinking, help those who are drinking with you; give way to everyone, and tolerate them. This is how you will do them good: don't impose your own evil moods on them!

103

Just as there are some bad actors who cannot sing on their own, but only as part of the chorus, so there are some men who cannot walk alone.

Man, if you have any value, try to walk on your own and speak to yourself, instead of hiding in a chorus! Spend your time thinking; look around you; do your best to discover your true nature!

104

So you say you would like to win at the Olympic Games. Yes, but think of what it will mean, what the consequences will be; then, and only then, try it–if it will be good for you. You will have to show discipline, diet, lay off fancy food, exercise at set times, whether it's hot or cold; stop drinking cold water and give up wine. In a word, you will have to give yourself completely into the control of your trainer, as though he were a doctor.

Then at the time of the competition, you will be thrown to the ground, you might dislocate your arm, sprain your ankle, have to swallow dirt, be struck with a whip–and despite all this you might not win. Weigh up what it will cost you, and then, if you still want to, try being a wrestler. If you don't then you will just be like a pack of children playing at being wrestlers, then at being gladiators; then they start pretending to play trumpets and to be actors, depending on what they seem. You are just the same: by turns you are a wrestler, gladiator, philosopher, orator and you don't fully commit to any of them. You are like an ape, copying what you see, never sticking with one thing; once you get used to something you get bored with it. This is because you never thought about it before you started, you never viewed it from every angle; you made your choice without thinking; the fire of your desire quickly died out.…

My friend, first think what it is you want to do, and then what you are able to cope with. If you want to be a wrestler, think about your shoulders, your thighs, your loins–not all men are shaped for the same purpose. Can you be a philosopher while you act as you do? Can you go on eating like this, drinking, letting your anger and annoyance get the better of you? No, you must be vigilant, you must work; you must overcome certain desires; you must abandon familiar friends, let your slave despise you, be mocked by those who encounter you, and take the lowest position in all areas of public life.

So weigh up all these things fully, and then, if you want to, start working; if you're willing to pay this price you will gain freedom, tranquillity and calm without passion.

105

Somebody who hasn't had music lessons is like a child music is concerned; someone who hasn't been taught to read is like a child in terms of learning; someone who hasn't been taught philosophy is like a child in life.

Can you gain anything from the sort of men? Yes, you can gain from every man.

"What, even from someone who just criticises everyone?"

Well, tell me what benefit the wrestler gets from the person who trains him? The greatest benefit of all: he builds up my endurance, he teaches me to control my temper, he teaches me to be gentle. You deny it. What, this man who grabs me by the neck, slaps around my shoulders and loins, does me good... but the person who trains me to keep my temper does me no good? This shows you what it's like not to know how to learn from men! Is my neighbour a bad man? He is bad to himself, but he is good to me: he teaches me to keep my temper, to be gentle. Is my father bad? He is bad to himself, but good to me. This is like the rod of Hermes; they say that you can touch what you like with it, and it will turn to gold. No, bring whatever you want and I will change it into something good. Bring me sickness, death, poverty, criticism, put me on trial for my life–through using this rod of Hermes it shall become profitable.

So until the right opinions have been firmly established in you, and you have become strong enough protect yourself, I advise you to be careful about mixing with those who are uneducated. Otherwise the things which you have learnt in School will gradually melt and disappear like wax in the sun. While your feelings are still like wax, keep them somewhere out of the sun.

108

We must approach this matter differently; it is a great and mystical thing; it is not common, and not every man has it. Wisdom on its own will not be enough to look after young men: a man needs to be prepared, to have a talent for the job, and certain physical qualities. Above all, he must have been appointed by God Himself to undertake the job; He appointed Socrates to demonstrate errors, Diogenes to issue reproofs, and Zeno to give positive instruction. You're like someone who wants to set up as a doctor with just a stock of drugs! You neither know nor care how they should be used.

109

If the only thing which pleases you is abstract principles, sit down and mull over it quietly, but don't call yourself a philosopher, and don't let others call you that either. You should say, he is in error, because my desires and instincts have not changed. I stick with the same way of life, and I haven't changed the way I deal with the world.

110

When a friend who was inclined to the views of the Cynics asked Epictetus what sort of person a true Cynic should be, asking him to outline the philosophy for him, he answered: "We will take our time thinking over that. For the moment I'll just say this: if a man devotes himself to such an important matter without the help of God, then God will be angry with him. The thing which he desires will just bring public shame upon him. Even when a man finds himself in a pleasant house, he doesn't step forward and say, 'I must be the master here!' If he does the Lord of the house will notice him and, seeing him insolently giving orders, he will drag him out and punish him. This is also the case in this great city and in the world. Here there is also a Lord who orders everything:

"You are the sun! In your orbit you have
The power to order the years and the seasons;
To make the fruits of the earth grow

And increase, the winds blow and drop;
You can as you wish
Warm up the bodies of men; go and make
Your orbit, and so bring your warmth to all of us,
From the highest to the lowest!

"You can lead an army against Troy; be
Agamemnon!"

"You can fight Hector in single combat; be Achilles!"

"But if Thersites had stepped forward and demanded
that he rule the whole army, he would have been
refused, or if he had been given it it would only have
led to his humiliation in front of everyone."

111

Other people might hide themselves with walls and
houses, when they do these sorts of things, and keep
themselves in the dark–yes, they have many tricks to
keep themselves in. Another one may close his door
and put a guard on his room to say, if anyone comes,
he has gone out! Is not available! But a true Cynic
will not do this; instead of that, he must use modesty
as his protection, otherwise he will the shamed, naked
under the open sky. Modesty is his house, his door,
the slave that guards his room, his darkness!

112

Death? Let it come when it wants, even if it just attacks a fraction of the whole. Run, you tell me, run! But where shall I run to? Can any man send me outside the limits of the world? It can't happen! And wherever I go, I will still find the Sun, the Moon and stars; I will find dreams, omens, and speak with the Gods!

113

Furthermore the true Cynic must recognise that he has been sent as a messenger from God to men, to show them that they are wrong about good and evil. They look for them where they cannot be found, and do not consider where they actually are. Like Diogenes when he was brought before Philip after the Battle of Chaeronea, the Cynic must remember that he is a spy. He really is a spy, charged with reporting what things are on the side of mankind, and what is against him. And when he has carefully looked at everything, he must come back with an accurate report, he mustn't be terrified into saying that those who are not enemies are enemies, nor should he be disturbed or confused by anything he observes.

114

How can it be that somebody who has nothing, no
fancy clothes, no house, no home, no one to care for
them, no servant, no city, can still live peaceful and
happy? God has sent you a man to demonstrate
clearly to you that this can happen. Look at me! I
don't have a house or possessions or servants: I sleep
on the ground, I have no wife, no children, no roof
over my head–just the Earth and sky and a single
ragged cloak. Yet what are my lacking? Am I not
immune to sorrow and fear? Am I not free? Have I
ever accused mankind or God or anything? When
have I accused anyone? Have any of you seen me
looking sad? How to treat those people who you stand
in awe of? Don't I regard them the same as slaves?
Who when he sees me doesn't think that he is looking
at his master and his king?

115

Think more carefully: know yourself: take advice
from God: don't try anything without him!

116

"But to marry and bring up children," said the young man, "does the Cynic think that this is one of the main tasks of mankind?"

Give me a nation of wise men, Epictetus answered, and perhaps not one of them would lightly become a Cynic. Why would he choose that way of life? However, supposing he does, there's nothing to stop him marrying or bringing up children. His wife would be the same sort of person as himself, and so would her father; and his children will be brought up the same way.

But the way things are at the moment, with society being like an army in battle, shouldn't a Cynic be free of all destruction and give himself over completely to the service of God, so that he can pass freely amongst men, not tied down to duties or relationships as ordinary men are? For if he does not do those duties, he will sacrifice the reputation of being a good and true man, and if he does do them, that prevents him being the messenger, the spy, the Herald of the Gods!

117

You ask me if a Cynic should be involved in government. You fool, can you think of a nobler government than the one he is involved in now? Do you think that a man should step out in the Athenian parliament and talk about revenue and supplies, when his job is to talk to all men, Athenians, Corinthians and Romans alike, not about supplies and revenue, or peace and war, but about happiness and misery, prosperity and adversity, slavery and freedom?

Are you asking whether a man who has being involved in such things should become involved with provincial government? Ask me if he should rule over people, and I will answer you again, fool, what greater power could he have than what he already has?

118

A man like this needs to treat his body in certain ways. If he looks consumptive, thin and pale, what he says won't carry the same authority. He must not only show the uneducated his soul, to demonstrate that one can be a good man without all the things which they admire, he must also show them, with his body, that a plain and simple life lived under the open sky doesn't do a man any harm. "Look at me, I am the proof of this, and so is my body." Diogenes used to go about looking very healthy, and men were drawn to pay attention to him just by the condition of his body. But if a Cynic is pitied, then he seems like a beggar; everyone turns away and is offended by him. And he shouldn't look slovenly either, so that men won't be repulsed by him in that way either; on the contrary, he should make sure that his rough appearance is both clean and attractive.

119

Kings and tyrants have armed guards which they used to punish certain people, although it is them themselves who are evil. But the Cynic gets the same power from conscience, not from weapons and guards. When he knows that he has watched over and worked on behalf of mankind; that he went to sleep pure, and woke up even purer; at his thoughts were those of a Friend of the Gods, a servant, but one who takes part in the government of the Supreme God, that he is always saying: "O God and destiny, leaves me!" as well as, "If this is the will of God, let it happen!"

If he knows all that, then why should he be afraid to speak boldly to his own family, to his children–to everyone related to him!

120

Does a philosopher ask people to come and listen to him? Doesn't he rather attract the people who will benefit from hearing him and, just as the sun warms them and food keeps them going? What doctor advertises for men to come and be cured? (Although I hear that nowadays the doctors at Rome do advertise for patients–in my day one would ask the doctor for treatment, not the other way round) I ask you to come and hear that you are in a bad way; that the thing you should pay most attention to is the last thing you look at; that you don't know good from evil, and in short you are a hopeless wretch; this would be fine advertising! But unless you get this message from the philosopher, both the speaker and his speech are worthless.

<hr />

121

The school of a philosopher is a surgery; when you go in you should feel pain, not pleasure. Because when you go in, not one of you is whole. Someone has a dislocated shoulder, another has an abscess; a third suffers from discharge, a fourth has headaches. So should I sit down and give you pretty sentiments and empty displays, so you can applaud me and leave, with none of your illnesses the slightest bit better? Is this what young men have to leave their homes for, leave behind their parents, their friends, their family and their wealth just to cheer on your empty phrases?

122

If anyone is unhappy, he should remember that he has made himself unhappy. God created all men to enjoy happiness and good things.

123

Will we never grow up–will we never listen to what philosophy teaches us (unless perhaps it has been ringing in our ears like the words of the hypnotist):

This world is one great city, and it is made of a single substance: there must be a certain time when one thing gives place to another; some people must die so that others can succeed; some must move and some must stay: but all things should be friends–first God, then men, nature has bound them together.

124

The hero did not weep or sorrow that he would be leaving his children to be orphans. He knew that no man is an orphan, because God the Father cares for everyone eternally. He hadn't just heard that Almighty God is the father of men: he actually believed it, and in everything he did he always kept his eyes fixed on him. So wherever he went, he could be happy.

125

Don't you know that this is a war? One man has a duty to be on guard, another must go out to scout around, a third one goes out to fight; they can't all be in one place, and even if they could it would be helpful. But you, instead of doing as your commander orders you, complain if you are asked to do anything more difficult than usual. You don't understand how your complaining is bringing down the army, as much as you can. If everyone followed your example, nobody would dig a trench, nobody would build ramparts around the camp, nobody would keep watch, or put himself in danger. Everyone would be useless as a soldier… this is the case here. Every life is a war, a long and varied one. You must do your duty as a soldier, and obey everything your commander orders: if it is possible, you should try and think what he wants you to do, so that there is no difference between your actions and what he would order.

Have you forgotten again? Don't you know that a
good man does nothing for the sake of appearances,
he does it because he wants to do right?

"So there is no reward?"

Reward! Are you looking for a greater reward than a
good man can have by doing the right thing? But at
the great games you don't ask if there was more
reward; you regard the crown for the winner as being
a good enough prize. So do you think it's such a
worthless thing, to be a good man, and to be happy?

127

It doesn't do you any good to be caused unhappiness
by anyone. It is better to be happy with everyone, and
especially with God, who made us for this purpose.

128

What, did Diogenes not love any man, that person who was so gentle, such a great friend of mankind that he was quite happy to suffer physically for the common good? But how did he love them? In a fashion appropriate for a Minister of the Supreme God, caring for men and obeying God's orders.

129

Nature has made me for my own good, not to suffer.

130

Remember that the person whom you love is mortal, that what you love does not belong to you; it is given to you from now, not for ever without change, it is given to you like figs or a bunch of grapes at the proper season of the year…

"But these are frightening words."

What, how can you call something frightening unless it is actually evil? Cowardice is evil, if you like, and meanness of spirit, and sorrowing and mourning, and shamelessness…

But I beg you, don't call something frightening when it signifies something natural: you might as well call harvesting the corn frightening; that means that the corn will be destroyed, but not the world! You might as well say it is evil when a leaf falls; that you should have dried figs in place of fresh ones, that grapes should be made into raisins. All these are changes from one state into another. They are not destruction, there is order and sense in it. It is like leaving home, just a small change; death is like that, a greater change, from what you are now, not into nothing, but into something different.

"Will I cease to exist?"

You will not; you will exist, but you will be something different, something the world needs. You didn't choose when to be born, you were born when the world needed you.

131

So a good true man, remembering who he is and where he came from, who fathered him, only cares about how he can do his duty properly and obediently to God.

Do you want me to carry on living? Then I will live, as a free and dignified man, as you would wish me to be. For you have taken away all constraints on my life. But do you now have no further need for me? I thank you! Up until now I stayed for your sake, for no other reason: and now I shall leave in obedience to you.

"How will you leave?"

I say again, as you would like me to; as a free man, as your servant, as someone who listens to what you order, and what you forbid.

132

Whatever place or post you give me, I would rather die a thousand deaths and, as Socrates put it, then deserved it. And where do you want me to go? To Rome or Athens? To Thebes or to a desert island? Just remember me when I am there! If you send me where a man cannot live as nature intended, I will leave; not out of disobedience to you, but as though you had given the order for me to leave. I am not deserting you—far be it from me to do that! It's just that I would have seen that you no longer have need of me.

133

If you are in Gyaros, don't dwell on life in Rome, and all the pleasure it gave you to live there, and everything you will find when you go back. What you should focus on is how someone living in Gyaros can live there like a strong man. And if you are living in Rome, then don't keep thinking about what it's like in Athens, focus solely on how you should live in Rome.

Finally, add this to your list of pleasures; the pleasure which comes from knowing that you are obeying the will of God.

134

To a good man there is nothing which is evil, either in life or death. If God does not give you food, isn't he just, like a wise commander, sounding the signal for retreat? I obey his orders, speaking well of my commander, and praising what he does. I came here on his orders, and I leave when he wants me to; and while I was alive it was my task to sing praise to God!

135

You should think of the fact that the main cause of all evil to man, and cause of low and cowardly behaviour, is not death, but the fear of death.

So I beg you to harden yourself against this fear; use all your thoughts, your exercises and you're reading to do this. Then you will know that this is how men become free.

136

The person who lives in the way he wants to live is free; no one can commit violence against them, nobody can hold him back or order him: his wishes and his desires are always fulfilled, he never takes a wrong step. So who would want to live in error? Nobody. Who would want to live deceived and likely to fall, unjust, intemperate, whining at his fate? Nobody. So no wicked man lives in the way he wants to, and so he is not free.

137

This is how the more cautious traveller behaves. He hears that there are robbers on the road. He won't go out alone, he will wait for an ambassador, a queastor or a proconsul to go with him. He will join his party and so get through safely. This is what the wise man does as he moves through the world. There are many robbers and tyrants, many storms and dangerous waters, a man can lose everything he holds dearest. What shall he do for safety–how shall he get through without being attacked? What companion shall he seek out to protecting? Some sort of wealthy man, a consul? How will I benefit if he is robbed and starts crying out and weeping? What if my fellow traveller turns on me and robustly? What shall I do? I shall become a friend of Caesar's! If I am with him nobody will do me any wrong! Firstly, what indignities I will have to suffer to become his friend! How many robbers there will be waiting to attack me! And if I succeed, Caesar is just a mortal man. What if I offend him, where shall I run to get away from him? Into the wilderness? Won't illness be waiting for me there? So what should I do? Can't I find a fellow traveller who is honest, loyal, strong and ready to fight off ambushes? So the wise man realises that if he wants to get through safely, he has to ally himself to God.

138

"What do you understand it to means, to attach himself to God?"

That he should want what God wants; and that he
should not want what God does not want.

"So how can this happen?"

He should consider what God does, and how he rules.

139

And do you, who has been given everything by another, sulk and blame the Giver, if he takes anything away from you? Why, who are you, and why are you here? Wasn't it him who showed you the light, who gave you fellow workers, and senses, and the power of reasoning? And how did he bring you into the world? Didn't he put you here as someone who is born to die, as someone who is sent to live out his earthly life in some little box of flesh, to see how he governs and to share with him for a little while a place in his great Festival Procession? So now whilst you were allowed you have seen his solemn feast and assembly; won't you leave gladly, when he calls you, praising and giving thanks for what you have seen and heard? "No, I wanted to stay longer at the Festival." Well, the priests would like to have their ceremonies go on longer; perhaps the crowd at the Great Games would like to see more wrestlers. But the Solemn Assembly is finished! Come away, leave with gratitude and modesty–make way so that others can live just as you have.

140

Why are you so greedy? Why are you so unreasonable? Why be a burden to the world? "Yes, but I want my wife and children with me." What, do they belong to you, and not to the One who gave them to you, the one who made you? So give up what doesn't belong to you: give it to the one who is greater than you. "No, but why did he bring me into the world on these conditions?" If it doesn't suit you, then leave! He doesn't need spectators who moan about their lot! He needs people who will join in with the feast, who will add their voices to the other men so that the applause will be greater, and so that the Great Assembly will be praised with hymns and songs. But He won't mind seeing wretched and fearful people being absent from the feast, for when they were there, they didn't behave as if they were at a feast, nor did they do the job they should have done; they moaned as if they were in pain, and they complained about their fate, their fortune and their companions. They didn't realise what they have been given, they didn't realise what powers they had been given for a very different purpose–generosity, nobility, strength and freedom!

141

So, are you free? A man might ask. I swear to God, I long and pray for freedom! But I can't look my masters straight in the face; I still value my poor body; I still care very much about keeping it whole and healthy.

But I can show you a free man, so that you don't have to keep looking for an example. Diogenes was free. Why was that? Not because he was born free (for in fact he was not), but because he was free himself. He had rid himself of every aspect of slavery, and it was impossible for anyone to make him into a slave. He was very loosely attached to everything possessions, he would rather. If you had stolen his let you take them away than bother to follow you to get them back–even if it had been one of his limbs, or perhaps his whole body; he had the same attitude to his relatives, friends and his country. He knew where they had come from, who had sent them to him and on what terms he welcomed them. His true ancestors, the Gods, his true country, he would never have abandoned; nor would he let any man be better than him at obeying and submitting to the gods or in being glad to die for the other. He was always thinking of the fact that everything that happens comes from there, and happens for the benefit of his true country, and is directed by the one who rules it.

142

Think about this–these beliefs, these words: fix your eyes on these examples, if you want to be free, if you are determined to get it, knowing what it's worth. How is it any surprise if you buy such a great thing for such a high price? For the sake of what men think of as freedom, some will hang themselves, some will throw themselves off cliffs; yes, in times past whole cities became completely extinct for it, and yet you begrudge God taking back what he has given you when he asked for it in exchange for true, certain and unbreakable freedom? Won't you learn, as Plato instructed, to tolerate not only death but torture, exile, whipping–in a word, will give up everything that doesn't belong to you? Otherwise you will be a slave amongst slaves, even if you were voted Consul ten thousand times, even if you were Emperor. You shall learn how true what Cleanthes said is, that although what philosophers say might not agree with what the world thinks, they have reason on their side.

143

When he was asked the best way for a man to give pain to his enemy, Epictetus replied, "By trying to live as nobly as possible himself."

144

I am free, I am a friend of God, I am ready and willing to obey him. I can't give any value to anything else, not my own body, nor my possessions, nor my status, nor my reputation, or anything else. He does not want me to value these things. If he had wanted to, he would have made those things central to my well-being. But he has not done so: so I cannot disobey a single one of his orders. At all times you must hold on to that which is good for you, but whatever else is given to you you should only hold on to as much as is reasonable, be happy with what you have. Otherwise you will suffer failure, bad luck, setbacks and difficulties. These are the laws made by God–these are his rules; these are what a man should explain and interpret; these are what he should obey, not the laws of Masurius and Cassius.

145

Don't just think that love of power and wealth makes us slaves to others, even love of peace, leisure, travel–learning in general, it doesn't matter what the external thing is–to place a value on it is to put yourself under the control of another person. What is the difference between wanting to be a senator, and wanting not to be one: dying to be in office and dying to be released from office? What is the difference between crying out, 'Alas, I don't know what to do, I am so tied to my books I can't move!' And crying out, 'Alas, I have no time to read!' as if the book wasn't something outside you and outside your will, just as office and power and influence with great men are.

Or, tell me, what reason have you for wanting to read? If all you want is to get pleasure from it, or to gain some scrap of knowledge, you are just a poor spiritless knave. But if you want to study for the right reasons, what else could they be other than ways of gaining a life of tranquillity and serenity? If your reading doesn't bring this serenity, what good is it? "No, it does bring me that," he says, "and that is why I am complaining that I have been deprived of it." What sort of serenity is it that can be stopped by any passerby? I say it is something that can't just be disturbed by the Emperor or the Emperor's favourite, you can lose it when a raven croaks or a piper plays, when you have a touch of fever or a thousand things like that! Whereas there is no more certain indicator of a serene life than that it can keep moving forward, unimpeded.

If you have completely rejected spite and speaking about things, or have at least managed to reduce it: if you have rejected rashness, swearing, drunkenness, laziness: if what used to move you no longer moves you, or doesn't move you in the same way–then you can celebrate everyday, today because you have done this thing well, tomorrow that thing. How much better a reason is this for giving sacrifice than just giving it because you have become a consul or prefect?

These things come to you from yourself and from the gods: just remember who it is that gave them to you– who they were given to and for what reason. If you keep meditating on this, do you have to question where you will find happiness? Where you will do as God wishes? Aren't all Gods the same in all places; don't they always see what's happening everywhere?

God has granted this inner freedom to every man. These are the principles that bring love to a house, stability to a city, peace amongst nations, teaching a man to be grateful to God and to be able to happily reject external things which he knows don't belong to him and are not worth trying to gain.

149

If you search for truth, you won't try to win by every method possible; and when you have discovered the truth, you don't need to worry about losing.

150

What is this foolish talk? How can I claim that I am on the right path, if I'm not satisfied with what I am but always anxious about what I am supposed to be?

151

God has made everything in the world, in fact the world itself, free-flowing and perfect, and all its parts work together. No other creature is capable of understanding the way in which he rules it, but having reason men have the ability to think of all these things. They can consider that not only are they parts of the world, but what part they are, and how proper it is for different parts to be sacrificed for the sake of the whole. This is not all. Having been made naturally noble, generous and free, he can see that the things which surround him are of two sorts. Some work freely and are controlled by the will. Others do not, and depend on the will of other men. So if he puts his own good, his own best interests, just in things which are free-flowing and in his power, he will be free, tranquil, happy, unharmed, noble hearted and pious; he will give thanks to God for all things, never complaining about whatever happens, never blaming anything. If he places his reliance on external things, which are not controlled by his will, he will experience obstacles, he will be the slave of those who have control over the things he desires and fears; he will have to be impious, for he will be complaining that he has been badly treated by God; he must be unfair, because he will always be trying to get more than he deserves; he will have to be a mean and miserable man.

152

So whom shall I be afraid of? The lords of the bedchamber, in case they would shut me out? If they find me wanting to come in, let them shut me out, if they want.

"Then why do you come to the door?"

Because I think it is right and proper to take part in the play, as long as it lasts.

"So in what way are you shut out?"

Because, unless they let me in, I do not choose to go in: all I want is just what happens. I value what God wants more than what I want. I will stick with him as his minister and servant; I will move in the same way, have the same desires, in short my will is his will. Only those who want to force their way in can be shut out; being shut out does not exist for me.

153

But what does Socrates say? "One man takes pleasure in improving his land, another one gets pleasure from his horses. My pleasure comes from seeing myself get better every day."

People dress according to the work they do; a craftsman gets his name from his craft, not from the clothes he wears. This is why Euphrates was right when he said, "For a long time I tried to hide the fact that I was living the life of a philosopher, and this did me a lot of good. Firstly, I knew that the things which I did right were done for my own sake, not for the sake of those watching me. I ate properly–I kept that to myself; I walked smoothly and steadily, I kept my face composed and calm–and that was just between me and God. As I was fighting alone, I was only risking myself. If I did anything wrong or shameful, I didn't do any harm to the cause of philosophy; nor did I do the public any harm by showing them and admitted philosopher doing wrong. So those who didn't know what I was doing were amazed that although I spent all my life talking with philosophers, I was not a philosopher myself. And what is wrong with the philosopher of being known by his actions, instead of by external signs and symbols?"

Firstly you must learn how to hide what you are; for a little while just look for wisdom by yourself. This is how fruit grows; first of all the seed must be planted in the ground for a little while, it must be hidden there and grow slowly, so that it can reach maturity. If the era grows before the stalk does, it is imperfect–something from the garden of Adonis*. You are like that sorry plant; you have blossomed too soon: you will wither away with the winter cold!

*Worshippers of Adonis would plant herbs which sprouted and died quickly, which they would then use in their ceremonies of mourning for the death of the God of vegetation.

156

Firstly, reject the life that you are leading now: but when you have rejected it, do not despair of yourself–don't be like those mean-spirited ones who, once they have decided they are wrong, give up completely and let themselves be washed away in the flood, as it were. No; be like the wrestling teachers. Has the boy fallen? "Get up," they say, "wrestle again, until you become stronger." That is how you should be. You should know there is nothing easier to control than the human soul. All you need is your will, and the job is done; the soul as been put on the proper path. The other side of the coin is that if you neglect your work for a moment, all is lost.

157

A man shows what he is in a crisis. So when the crisis comes to you, remember that God, like someone who trains wrestlers, has given you a rough and strong opponent. "Why has he done that?" you ask. So that you can triumph at the Great Games. But without work and sweat this cannot happen!

158

If you want to make progress, don't worry about seeming foolish and not understanding worldly things. Don't care about people thinking you know anything. If anyone thinks you're important, don't trust yourself.

159

Remember that you should behave in life as if you are at a banquet. Have any of the dishes being served come to you? Put out your hand and help yourself with moderation. Does it go past you? Don't try and stop it. Has it not come yet? Don't start longing for it, wait until it gets to you. This is how you should deal with children, with wives, with politicians, with money–and one day you will be ready to share the Banquets of the Gods. But if you don't even touch what is placed in front of you, but hate it, then you will not only share the Banquets of the Gods, but also their Empire.

160

Remember that you are an actor in a play, and you have the part which the author chooses for you, whether it is long or short. If he wants to make you play a beggar, a ruler, or a simple citizen, then it is your job to play your part properly. What you have to do is play the part which has been given to you, well: someone else chooses the part.

161

Think daily about death and exile, and everything else that men think is terrible, but especially death. Then you will never think a mean thought, and you will not covet anything which you should not.

162

Just as a target is not put up to be missed, there is no such thing as natural evil produced in the world.

163

It is certain that proper respect for the gods consists mainly in thinking properly about them–that they exist, and that they govern the universe with goodness and justice, and that your job is to obey them and to bow down to them under any circumstances; you should cheerfully agree to whatever happens to you, in the certainty that it has happened and been planned by a Perfect Intelligence. In this way you will never find fault with the Gods, and you will never accuse them of neglecting you.

164

Don't waste any time in adopting a certain type of
character and behaviour when you're on your own
and with others. In general be silent, or only say what
is necessary and don't use too many words to say it.
However, when appropriate, we shall have a little
talk, though not about the usual topics of gladiators,
horse races and athletes, or the eternal talk about food
and drink. Above all we should avoid speaking about
other people, either good or bad, or comparing them
with others.

If you can, turn the conversation of those you with
round to what you would be thinking of if you were
on your own. But if you find yourself amongst
strangers and foreigners and unable to escape, say
nothing.

165

You should not laugh too long, too often, nor without
restraint.

166

if possible, you should completely refuse to take an oath, if not then only take those which are absolutely impossible to avoid.

167

You should avoid banquets of uneducated men and outsiders. But if you have to join in, don't let your guard down for a moment, in case you slip into evil ways. You can rest assured that however pure a man is, if his associates are impure he cannot escape being stained by them.

168

Take the bare minimum that your body needs, in terms of meat, drink, clothes, housing and servants. But reject everything which is luxurious or showy.

169

If you're told that somebody has spoken badly of you, don't defend yourself against what he says, say, "Surely he didn't know all my other faults, otherwise he wouldn't just have mentioned these!"

170

If you visit anyone who is powerful, remember that you might not find him in, that you might not be admitted, that the door might be slammed in your face, that he might not care about you. If in the face of all this, it is your duty to go, put up with what happens and never say, "It was not worth the trouble!" That would be the behaviour of a foolish and uneducated man who allows external things to affect him.

171

When you are in company avoid frequent and
unnecessary talk about your own actions and the
dangers you have faced. However much you might
enjoy describing the risks you have run, others might
not enjoy hearing about your adventures so much.
Avoid making people laugh also, once you start that it
is easy to become foolish and lose the respect your
neighbours have for you. It is also dangerous to talk
in a vulgar fashion. When this sort of thing happens,
if you get a chance, tell the speaker off. If you don't
get a chance, at least go silent, red in the face and
look annoyed, to show that you don't like the subject.

172

Once you have decided that something ought to be
done, and you're doing it, don't try and hide the fact
that you are doing it, even if most people would think
that you are wrong. If you are not doing the right
thing, then stop doing it; if you are, why worry about
misguided criticism?

173

It is a sign of a small man to spend too long on bodily matters, such as taking a long time over exercise, spending a long time eating, a long time drinking, a long time performing other bodily functions. These things should take a back seat to your efforts to gain knowledge.

174

Everything has two handles, one of which can be used to carry it, the other one cannot. If your brother sins against you, don't grab the handle of injustice, because that cannot be used to handle it: take hold of the handle which tells you that he is your brother, the friend of your youth, and so you will be able to bear it.

175

Never describe yourself as a philosopher or talk much too uneducated men about principles, but act like a philosopher, act from principles. So at a banquet, don't discuss how people should eat, but eat in the right way. Remember that Socrates did this and completely avoided showing off. Men would come to him asking him to recommend them to philosophers, and he would take them there himself–that was how little he cared about the ignored. So if uneducated men start talking about principles, for the most part remain silent. You would be taking a great chance of throwing up what you haven't understood. When a man tells you that you know nothing and that does not annoy you, you can be sure you are on the right track.

176

When you have learned to satisfy your body without much cost, do not pride yourself on that, and if you only drink water, don't keep saying, I only drink water! If you ever want to improve your endurance and suffer hardship, do not boast about it!

177

When a man is proud of the fact that he can understand and interpret the writings of Chyrsippus, say to yourself:

If Chyrisippus hadn't written in an obscure way, this fellow would have nothing to be proud of. But what is it I want? To understand Nature, and to do as she wishes! So I ask who can interpret her. Hearing that Chrysippus can, I go to him. But it seems I can't understand his writings. So I look for someone to explain them. So far there's nothing for me to be proud of. But once I've found an interpreter, I still have to do as he says. That's the only thing to be proud of. But if all I admire is the interpretation, what have I become; just a commentator, not a lover of wisdom. The only difference is that I am commenting on Chrysippus instead of Homer. So if someone asks me to read Chrysippus to them it generally makes me blush, because what I do doesn't accord with what he writes.

178

When you are at a feast, remember that you are entertaining both the body and the soul. What you give to the body will soon disappear; what you give to the soul stays with you forever.

179

When you are at a meal, make sure that there are not more servants than guests. It is ridiculous for a whole crowd of servants to be dancing attendants on half a dozen chairs.

180

You should share what is going on with your servants, both in terms of preparation and in enjoying the feast. If you find that difficult, remember that you are not tired and being served by people who are; you are eating and drinking in front of those who do neither; you are talking in front of those who have to stay silent; you are comfortable in front of those who have to stay formal. If you share with them then no sudden anger will make you behave unreasonably, and nobody will be irritated by your harsh behaviour.

181

When Xanthippe was scolding Socrates for not making much preparation to entertain his friends, he answered, "If they are friends of ours they won't care about it; if they aren't friends, then we won't care about them!"

182

When Epictetus was asked who is rich, he answered, "The satisfied man."

183

Favorinus tells us how Epictetus would also say that there were two things far worse than any others, the inability to show endurance and the inability to to show restraint, so that we don't patiently tolerate things which we should suffer nor do we resist pleasures which we should not indulge in. "So," he carried on, "if a man just remembers these two words, and makes sure that he follows them in ruling over himself, he will usually manage to avoid sin, and his life will be calm and serene." He meant the words, "Endurance and restraint."

184

At all times these thoughts should be kept in mind:

Lead me, O God, and you, O Fortune;
Whatever you have in mind for me
I shall follow bravely; if I don't want to
That would make me a coward, but I must still do it!

Again:

The man who does what he has to,
Is wise and knows what God desires.

And also:

Crito, if this is what God orders, let it happen. As for me,
Anytus and Meletus can certainly put me to death, but they can never injure me!

185

So we will be like Socrates when we can sing the praises of God when we are in prison.

186

It is hard to combine these two ideas, having the care
of someone affected by cirumstances and the daring
of someone who doesn't care about them. But it is
not impossible, otherwise happiness would be
impossible. We should behave as we do at sea.

"What can I do?" Choose your captain, your crew,
the day, the time. Then a sudden storm blows up.
What do I care? I've done my job. Everything is
down to someone else, the captain. The ship is
sinking. So what should I do? There is only one
thing I can do; I must drown without fear, without
crying out, without complaining to God, knowing that
what has been born must also die. I am not immortal,
I am a human being – one part of the whole, just as a
single hour is a part of the day. I must regard myself
as an hour of time, and my hour must pass.

187

And now we are sending you to Rome to see how
things are; but nobody sends a coward for a job like
that, someone who hears a noise and sees a shadow
and cries out, "The enemy is coming!"

So if you go now and come back to tell us,
"Everything at Rome is terrible, there is awful death,
exile, famine, slander; run, friends! The enemy are
on us!" we will answer, "Go away, and keep your
panic to yourself! We made a mistake sending a spy
like you. Diogenes, who went sent as a spy long
before you, brought back a very different report. He
said that death was not evil, for it doesn't even have
to bring shame. He says that fame is just the
worthless yelling of madmen. And what did this spy
tell us about pain, pleasure, need? That to be dressed
in sackcloth is better than any purple robe; that the
hard ground is the softest bed; and to prove all these
things he points out his own courage, unwavering
belief and freedom, along with his strong and healthy
body. "There is no enemy nearby," he cries,
"everything is perfectly peaceful!"

188

If a man has this peace – not the peace which Ceasar declares (how is it his to declare?), but the peace which God declares through reason, won't that be enough for him when he is alone, when he looks and thinks: now nothing evil can happen to me, for me there are no robbers, no earthquakes; everything is peaceful and tranquil for me; I can't be harmed by crowds, not in the city or out on the road, neither my neighbour or my friend can hurt me. Someone else gives me food, my clothes, has taught me how to think and know where all begins. When he no longer gives me what I need, that is because He is sounding the retreat, He has opened the door and is saying, Come! Where to? To nothing you need be afraid of, back to the friendly elements from which you came; whatever is in you of fire, back to fire; earth back to earth, water back to water, spirit back to spirit. There is no Hades, no mythical rivers of sighs or sorrow or fire; everything is full of spiritual and divine beings. When he thinks this a man is neither helpless nor alone when he looks on the universe!

When death comes, what do you want to be
discovered doing? If I could choose, I would want to
be found doing something truly humane, important,
good and noble. But if I'm not found doing
something that elevated, let me hope for this -
something nobody can block, that is certainly in my
power - that I will be discovered trying to better
myself; that I will be dealing with matters of the
senses wisely, finding my path to tranquility, and so
treating everything in life in the correct manner...

If death finds me like this, it will be enough for me to
stretch my arms out to God and say, "I have not
neglected the faculties which you gave me to
understand your rule. As far as I could, I have shown
my respect for you. See how I have used my senses,
the elemental ideas you gave me. Have I ever blamed
you for anything? Have I ever grumbled about
anything that happened, or wished it could be
different? Have I behaved in any way which
disturbed the balance of life? For you created me,
and I thank you for the things you have given me: it
was enough for me in the time you have given me.
Take them back and do what you want with them!
They were all yours, and you gave them to me." If a
man leaves his life feeling like this, isn't that enough?
What life has been better or more noble, and who
enjoys a happier death?